Build Your Dream Gaming PC 2024

A Complete Guide to Assembling, Optimizing, and
Maintaining Your Ultimate Setup for Beginners

Robert I. Grass

Disclaimer

The content in this guide is for informational purposes only. While every effort has been made to ensure the accuracy of the information, the author and publisher make no guarantees about its reliability or suitability for your specific needs.

By using this guide, you agree that the author is not responsible for any damages, losses, or issues that may arise from following the steps or recommendations outlined. If you are uncertain about any aspect of building a gaming PC, it is advised to seek professional assistance.

Table of Contents

Introduction

The process of building your own gaming PC is fun and rewarding, and it lets you make a system that fits your wants, tastes, and gaming style. Building your own gaming PC is the best way to make sure you get exactly what you want, whether you want better speed, a more immersive gaming experience, or just to feel good about putting your system together.

This book is meant to help you with every step of the process, from choosing the right parts to making your system run at its best.

Why Build a Gaming PC?

Performance is very important when it comes to games. For gamers, a PC can give you more power and flexibility than most pre-built systems. Building your own game PC is a good idea for the following reasons:

1. Making changes

You can use any parts you want when you build your own game PC instead of the ones that come already put together. You can pick out each part based on your income and gaming needs. Want the latest graphics card, a high-end engine, or more storage? It's all up to you.

2. Better Performance

Custom-built gaming PCs can offer superior speed compared to their off-the-shelf counterparts. With the right components, you can achieve higher frame rates, better graphics quality, and smoother gameplay, which makes a big difference in competitive gaming and overall enjoyment.

3. Upgradability

One of the biggest advantages of building your own gaming PC is the potential to upgrade individual components as technology improves. With pre-built systems, you might be stuck with a set configuration that doesn't allow for easy upgrades. A custom-built PC lets you swap out parts like the

GPU, RAM, or storage as needed, keeping your system current and powerful for years to come.

4. Cost-Effectiveness

While it's true that some high-end custom gaming PCs can be pricey, you can also build a powerful gaming machine without breaking the bank. By selecting the components that fit your price and performance needs, you can avoid paying for features or specifications you don't need. In many cases, building your own PC is more cost-effective than getting a pre-built one with similar specs.

5. Satisfaction and Learning

The process of making a gaming PC is an educational experience. You'll learn about the different components, how they work together, and how to fix when things don't go as planned. There's also a deep sense of satisfaction that comes from making something yourself, knowing that you built a system that's perfectly suited to your gaming needs.

Benefits of Customizing Your Setup

A customized gaming PC gives far more than just raw performance. Here are some specific perks of tailoring your setup to fit your style and needs:

1. Better Cooling and Longevity

Customizing your PC allows you to pick cooling solutions that are optimized for your components. Whether you're looking for liquid cooling for the best thermal management or air cooling for a budget-friendly setup, you have full control. This not only ensures that your PC runs cooler, but it can also extend the lifespan of your components by avoiding overheating.

2. Aesthetics and Personalization

A gaming PC is more than just a machine; it's a part of your personal area. Building your own allows you to choose a case that fits your style, from sleek minimalism to flashy RGB lighting sets. You can even match your build with your game setup, creating a cohesive and eye-catching aesthetic that fits your personality.

3. Optimized Gaming Experience

Whether you're gaming on a 1080p monitor or a 4K display, a custom gaming PC allows you to pick the components that best suit your desired gaming resolution and refresh rate. If you're into VR or competitive gaming, you can choose high-performance components that offer the smoothest, most immersive experience possible.

4. Reliability and Quality Control

When you hand-pick each component for your PC, you can favor quality and reliability over mass-produced parts. You get to choose reputable names and models that you trust, ensuring that your system is built with quality in mind. This can result in fewer issues down the line and a system that is more dependable generally.

5. Game-Specific Optimization

Different games have different system requirements, and with a custom build, you can tailor your system to run particular games at their best. If you're into graphically demanding titles like Cyberpunk 2077, or competitive FPS games like Fortnite, you can choose parts that are designed for those gaming experiences.

Overview of the Gaming Setup Process

Building and optimizing a gaming PC is an enjoyable and rewarding journey, but it requires a few key steps to ensure that your final setup offers the best experience. Here's a quick summary of the process:

1. Choosing the Right Components

The first step is picking the right components for your gaming PC. This includes choosing a processor (CPU), graphics card (GPU), memory (RAM), storage, motherboard, power source, and cooling system. Each component affects the overall performance of your PC, so it's important to study what will give you the best performance for your specific needs and budget.

2. Assembling the PC

Once you've chosen your components, it's time to put everything together. This step includes installing the CPU, RAM, GPU, storage, and other components into the motherboard and PC case. While it might seem daunting at first, assembling a gaming PC is actually quite simple when you break it down step by step. We'll help you through the process in detail, ensuring that your build is both functional and safe.

3. Optimizing the Gaming Setup

After the PC is assembled, you'll need to make sure it's optimized for games. This includes configuring BIOS settings, installing necessary drivers, adjusting system settings, and overclocking for added efficiency. We'll also explore how to optimize the visual and speed settings in your games to ensure smooth, high-quality gameplay.

4. Installing Accessories and Peripherals

A good game PC setup isn't just about the computer itself. To get the full experience, you'll need peripherals like a monitor, computer, mouse, headset, and controller. Choosing the right accessories to complement your build is key to maximizing comfort and performance during long game sessions.

5. Overclocking and Fine-Tuning

For gamers who want to push their system to the limit, overclocking can offer an extra boost in speed. Overclocking the CPU and GPU can provide higher frame rates and improved game performance, though it requires careful attention to cooling and system stability. We'll help you through the process of safely overclocking your system.

6. Maintenance and Troubleshooting

To keep your gaming PC in top shape, regular maintenance is important. This includes cleaning your PC, updating drivers, and trying your system for stability. If you experience problems down the road, we'll also walk you through basic troubleshooting techniques to help you fix common issues.

7. Updating and Upgrading Your Setup

Technology moves quickly, and part of having a gaming PC is staying current with hardware and software updates. Whether it's installing a new graphics card or upgrading your storage, this book will help you understand when and how to improve your PC to keep it running at its best.

This introduction sets the stage for everything that's to come in the following parts. It highlights the benefits of building your own game PC, explains why it's worth the effort, and provides an overview of the steps involved in creating your dream setup.

Chapter 1: Understanding Your Gaming Needs

It's essential to take a step back and think about your gaming needs before diving into the technical details of building your gaming PC. Since a gaming PC is highly customizable, the components you choose will depend heavily on the types of games you play, your budget, and which aspects of gaming matter most to you. Building a system that fits your specific needs ensures that you get the best performance, value, and longevity out of your setup.

This chapter will guide you through the essential questions you need to ask yourself to make sure your gaming PC is built around your personal gaming style and needs.

What Type of Games Do You Play?

The games you play have the most direct impact on the components you'll need. Not all games are made equal when it comes to hardware demands. Some require powerful graphics cards and CPUs, while others may not need as much working power. Knowing the types of games you play (or want to play) will help you decide where to allocate your budget for the best results.

1. Casual Games & Indie Titles

Casual games, puzzle games, and indie releases often don't require high-end hardware to run well. Games like Stardew Valley, Minecraft, or Among Us are not graphically demanding and can run easily on mid-range or even lower-end gaming PCs. If you're mainly playing these types of games, your goal should be a good CPU and sufficient RAM, but you don't need to overspend on a top-tier graphics card (GPU).

2. Competitive & Multiplayer Games

Games like Fortnite, Valorant, League of Legends, or Call of Duty place more demand on the GPU and CPU, especially in multiplayer modes where frame rates and response times can greatly affect gameplay. For these games, a strong GPU and CPU are essential for high frame rates (FPS) and smooth gameplay, especially if you're aiming to play at higher settings or resolutions like 1080p or 1440p.

3. AAA Titles & Open-World Games

AAA games like Cyberpunk 2077, Red Dead Redemption 2, and Assassin's Creed are resource-intensive and can push your PC to its limits. These games demand powerful GPUs and CPUs to create detailed graphics, complicated environments, and high-resolution textures. If you're planning on playing the latest and most demanding games at high levels or resolutions (4K gaming, for example), investing in high-end components such as a top-tier GPU (like the NVIDIA RTX series) and a multi-core CPU (like AMD Ryzen 7 or Intel i7) will be necessary.

4. Virtual Reality (VR) Games

If you plan to experience virtual reality gaming, it takes even more specialized hardware. VR gaming needs a high refresh rate and low latency to avoid motion sickness, so a high-performance GPU and a powerful CPU are important. VR headsets like the Oculus Rift, HTC Vive, or Valve Index come with their own set of system requirements, usually demanding at least a mid-range gaming PC to ensure smooth and immersive experiences.

Understanding the specific needs of the games you play will help you allocate your budget effectively.

There's no need to spend for high-end components if you're playing less demanding games, but if you want to experience the latest AAA games in all their glory, it's worth investing in powerful hardware.

Determining Your Budget and Priorities

Once you know what types of games you'll be playing, the next step is determining how much you're willing to spend. Your budget will play a crucial role in choosing which components to choose. Gaming PCs can range from $500 for an entry-level setup to $2,500 or more for a high-end build. Understanding your goals will help you get the best performance within your budget.

1. Entry-Level Builds (Budget: $500 - $800)

An entry-level gaming PC is great for casual gamers who don't mind playing on medium settings or lower resolutions. With this budget, you can build a system that can run many famous games like Fortnite, Minecraft, or League of Legends with ease. A solid GPU like the GTX 1650 or Radeon RX

580, paired with a decent quad-core CPU like the AMD Ryzen 3 or Intel Core i3, will offer satisfactory performance for these games.

2. Mid-Range Builds (Budget: $800 - $1,500)

A mid-range gaming PC can handle most current games at high settings, 1080p or even 1440p resolution. If you're playing competitive games or AAA titles but don't need ultra settings, a GPU like the NVIDIA RTX 3060 or AMD Radeon RX 6700 XT, combined with a powerful CPU like the AMD Ryzen 5 or Intel Core i5, will offer excellent performance. This amount also allows for better cooling systems and faster storage like an SSD.

3. High-End Builds (Budget: $1,500 - $2,500+)

A high-end gaming PC is made for gamers who want the absolute best experience, whether it's playing at 4K resolution, using virtual reality, or future-proofing for years to come. With this budget, you can buy top-of-the-line GPUs like the NVIDIA RTX 4080 or 4090, coupled with an octa-core CPU like the AMD Ryzen 7 or Intel Core i7/i9. You'll also have the ability to use advanced features like water cooling, custom RGB lights, and fast PCIe Gen 4 SSDs for lightning-fast load times.

4. Future-Proofing

If you want your gaming PC to last a few years without needing major upgrades, investing in higher-end components upfront might be a smart choice. A powerful CPU, plenty of RAM (16GB or more), and a high-performance GPU will ensure that your system can handle future games as technology improves, without requiring a full upgrade anytime soon.

The Role of Performance vs. Aesthetics

When building a gaming PC, there's a balance between speed and aesthetics. While performance is undeniably the most important element, the look of your gaming rig can also enhance your gaming experience. In fact, many gamers enjoy customizing the look of their PC with RGB lighting, sleek cases, and unique cooling solutions.

1. Performance First

Regardless of how sleek your game PC looks; performance should always come first. A powerful CPU, sufficient RAM, and a high-quality GPU are the core components that will determine how well your system plays games. If you're on a tight budget, focus on maximizing efficiency before splurging on cosmetic enhancements.

2. Aesthetics and Customization

Once you've got the speed down, you can consider adding some personal flair to your build. Features like RGB lighting, custom cases, tempered glass panels, and cable management can make your rig look powerful and unique. Customizing the appearance of your gaming PC can be as much fun as picking the components themselves, but always ensure that the aesthetics don't compromise airflow or cooling efficiency.

3. Cooling Solutions

Cooling is an important part of both function and aesthetics. If you're overclocking your system for better performance, having a strong cooling solution (like custom water cooling or high-quality air coolers) will keep your components from overheating. Cooling solutions are also an area where aesthetics can shine, with coolers having colorful LED lights or intricate tubing designs for a striking look.

Essential Features for a Gaming PC

There are certain features that every gaming PC should have to ensure an optimal experience, regardless of your game style or budget.

1. Graphics Processing Unit (GPU)

The GPU is the heart of any game PC. It handles all the graphical imagery that brings games to life. The stronger the GPU, the better the images and frame rates. If you're serious about gaming, investing in a powerful GPU like the NVIDIA RTX series or AMD's Radeon RX 6000 series is important.

2. Central Processing Unit (CPU)

The CPU is responsible for running the game's logic, processing commands, and handling background tasks. For games, you'll need a multi-core processor with high clock speeds. For most gamers, the AMD Ryzen 5 or Intel Core i5 will be sufficient, but competitive gamers may select Ryzen 7 or Intel Core i7/i9 for faster processing.

3. Memory (RAM)

A minimum of 16GB of RAM is recommended for most game setups today. RAM helps your system to multitask and ensures that games run smoothly without stuttering. Faster RAM can improve speed, but for most gamers, 16GB of DDR4 RAM will be more than enough.

4. Storage

Solid-State Drives (SSDs) are important for quick load times and a faster overall experience. A 500GB or 1TB SSD is great for installing your operating system and your favorite games. If you want extra storage for other programs or games, consider adding a larger HDD (Hard Disk Drive) or a secondary SSD.

5. Motherboard and Power Supply

The motherboard connects all your components, so it's important to choose one that supports your CPU and GPU while providing ample expansion options. A reliable power supply (PSU) ensures that your device gets consistent and stable power. Aim for a PSU with at least 80+ Bronze certification and suitable wattage for your build.

Understanding these important components and how they relate to your gaming needs will help you make the right decisions as you begin building your dream gaming PC. With the right components in place, you'll be on your way to enjoying games the way they were meant to be played—at their best.

Chapter 2: Essential Components for Your Gaming PC

When constructing your gaming PC, focusing on the key components is essential for achieving the desired performance and ensuring a seamless gaming experience. The graphics card, processor, and other parts all play significant roles in how your system will perform.

By understanding the importance of each component and how they work together, you can make smarter decisions when selecting the right parts. Whether your goal is to achieve high-end graphics, smooth frame rates, or a long-lasting setup, choosing the proper components is the crucial first step in building a powerful gaming machine.

CPU (Central Processing Unit)

The CPU is the heart of your gaming PC and plays a critical role in how your system works, both in and out of games. The CPU handles most of the computing tasks, such as executing instructions, handling game logic, and processing in-game actions that don't directly involve graphics.

While modern games rely heavily on the GPU for rendering visuals, the CPU is still vital for total system performance, especially in games with complex mechanics or simulations like strategy games, role-playing games (RPGs), or open-world titles.

Key Considerations:

1. Cores and Threads: The more cores and threads a CPU has, the better it can handle programming and parallel processing. For gaming, a quad-core CPU used to be enough, but today, most modern games gain from 6-core or 8-core processors. CPUs with multi-threading (such as Intel's Hyper-Threading or AMD's Simultaneous Multi-Threading) allow each core to handle more jobs simultaneously, improving performance in CPU-intensive games.

2. Clock Speed (GHz): The clock speed, measured in gigahertz (GHz), shows how fast the CPU can execute instructions. Higher clock speeds lead to faster processing. For gaming, a CPU with a clock speed of 3.5 GHz or higher is usually ideal, though the number of cores will often matter more than the raw clock speed in multi-threaded games.

3. Brand: Currently, the two top brands for gaming CPUs are Intel and AMD. Intel's Core i5 and i7 series, and AMD's Ryzen 5 and Ryzen 7 series, are particularly popular among gamers for their balance of speed and cost.

4. Intel: Intel's Core i5 or i7 (10th, 11th, or 12th Gen) provide great performance for gaming, with high clock speeds and good single-core performance, making them ideal for gaming.

o **AMD:** AMD's Ryzen 5 and Ryzen 7 CPUs offer great multi-core performance at a more affordable price. Ryzen CPUs usually outperform Intel in tasks that need more cores, such as video editing or streaming.

Recommended CPUs for Gaming:

- Intel Core i5-13600K or i7-13700K (12th Gen)
- AMD Ryzen 5 7600X or Ryzen 7 7700X

GPU (Graphics Processing Unit)

The GPU is often considered the most important component for gaming performance. The GPU renders the images and visuals in a game, translating game data into what you see on your computer. For graphically intense games like first-person shooters, racing games, or open-world adventures, a strong GPU is important for smooth, high-quality graphics.

Key Considerations:

1. VRAM (Video RAM): The amount of VRAM in your GPU controls how much graphical data can be stored and processed at once. For modern gaming, 8GB of VRAM is usually recommended, especially for higher-resolution displays (1440p or 4K).

2. Resolution & Refresh Rate: Your GPU should be chosen based on your gaming resolution (1080p, 1440p, or 4K) and the refresh rate of your monitor (60Hz, 144Hz, 240Hz, etc.). For instance, NVIDIA's RTX 3060 is ideal for 1080p gaming, while RTX 3080 or RTX 4090 are better suited for 4K gaming.

3. Ray Tracing and DLSS: Modern GPUs, especially from NVIDIA's RTX series, support Ray

Tracing (for realistic lighting and shadows) and DLSS (Deep Learning Super Sampling) (for better performance at high resolutions). These technologies improve visual quality without sacrificing frame rates.

Recommended GPUs for Gaming:

- NVIDIA GeForce RTX 3060 (for 1080p gaming)
- NVIDIA GeForce RTX 4070 (for 1440p gaming)
- NVIDIA GeForce RTX 4080 or RTX 4090 (for 4K games)

RAM (Random Access Memory)

RAM is the short-term memory of your PC, briefly storing data that the CPU and GPU need to access quickly while gaming. Having sufficient RAM allows your system to run smoothly without slowdowns, especially in memory-intensive tasks like gaming, multitasking, or running background apps while gaming.

Key Considerations:

1. Capacity: For gaming, 16GB of RAM is the sweet spot, allowing you to run current games without performance issues or slowdowns. Some professional gamers or streamers may benefit from 32GB of RAM, especially if they run other apps (like recording software or streaming programs) simultaneously.

2. Speed: RAM speed, measured in MHz, can slightly affect game performance. 3200MHz to 3600MHz is a good goal for most users. Faster RAM may help some games, especially those that rely on CPU performance, but it's not a game-changer for most gaming scenarios.

3. Dual Channel vs. Single Channel: RAM in dual-channel mode (using two sticks of RAM) offers better speed than single-channel, as it allows for faster data transfer between the CPU and RAM.

Recommended RAM for Gaming:

- Corsair Vengeance LPX 16GB (2x8GB) 3200MHz
- G.Skill Ripjaws V 16GB (2x8GB) 3600MHz

Storage (SSD vs. HDD) Storage is where your game

files, operating system, and other data are saved. While HDDs (Hard Disk Drives) have been the traditional storage solution, SSDs (Solid State Drives) are now the standard for gaming PCs due to their faster read/write speeds, reducing load times and enhancing total system performance.

Key Considerations:

1. SSD (Solid State Drive): An SSD greatly improves the speed of your system. Games saved on an SSD load faster, and Windows boot-up times are also much quicker. NVMe SSDs are even faster than SATA SSDs, offering lightning-fast speeds that make game installs and load times almost instantaneous.

2. Capacity: For gaming, a 500GB or 1TB SSD is usually recommended for fast storage of the operating system and the most-played games. For extra storage, you can pair it with a secondary HDD for storing larger game libraries or files that don't require quick access.

3. HDD (Hard Disk Drive): While slower, HDDs are still useful for storing non-essential files and older games that you don't mind waiting to start.

Recommended Storage for Gaming:

- Samsung 970 EVO Plus 1TB NVMe SSD
- Seagate Barracuda 2TB HDD (for extra storage)

Motherboard

The motherboard is the backbone that connects all of your components. It offers the slots, ports, and sockets where all the other components (CPU, GPU, RAM, etc.) are installed. Choosing the right motherboard is important for compatibility, performance, and future upgrades.

Key Considerations:

1. Form Factor: Motherboards come in different sizes (ATX, mATX, ITX). For gaming, an ATX motherboard is usually recommended due to its ample space for expansion and extra features.

2. Chipset: The chipset sets the features and capabilities of the motherboard. For Intel CPUs, you'll want a Z-series chipset (like Z590 for 11th Gen or Z690 for 12th Gen), and for AMD, look for an X570 or B550 chipset for future-proofing.

3. PCIe spots and Ports: Ensure your motherboard has enough PCIe spots for your GPU, sound cards, and other expansion cards. Additionally, consider USB ports, Ethernet, and Wi-Fi options for connectivity.

Recommended Motherboards:

- MSI MPG Z690 Carbon WIFI (for Intel)
- ASUS ROG Strix X570-E (for AMD)

Power Supply Unit (PSU)

The PSU is the component that gives power to all the other parts of your PC. It's important to choose a PSU that provides enough power for your components and has enough headroom for future upgrades.

Key Considerations:

1. Wattage: The PSU should provide enough wattage to run your system. A 650W to 750W PSU is sufficient for most mid-range game setups. If you plan to use high-end components or boosting, go for an 850W or 1000W PSU.

2. Efficiency ranking: Look for an 80+ Gold or better efficiency ranking. The higher the rating, the more energy-efficient the PSU, meaning less power is lost as heat.

Recommended PSUs:

- Corsair RM750x 750W 80+ Gold
- EVGA Supernova 850 G5 850W 80+ Gold

Cooling System

A cooling system is important for keeping optimal performance and longevity in your gaming PC. As your CPU, GPU, and other components work hard to render images and run processes, they generate heat. Without proper cooling, these components can overheat, which may lead to throttling (slowing down to avoid damage), system instability, or even lasting hardware damage.

Types of Cooling Systems:

1. Air Cooling: The most popular and budget-friendly option. It uses fans to move air and dissipate heat from the CPU, GPU, and other parts.

Air coolers can range in size, from compact single-fan coolers to large tower coolers with multiple fans. Air cooling is usually sufficient for most gaming builds, given you have good airflow in your case.

2. Liquid Cooling (Water Cooling): This method involves a liquid coolant moving through a closed loop that absorbs heat from the components. Liquid cooling is more efficient than air cooling, especially in high-performance systems, as it can handle more heat and keep temperatures lower. While usually more expensive and difficult to install, it's often used in systems where overclocking or heavy workloads are expected, or for a quieter system.

Key Considerations:

1. Thermal Paste: Essential for heat movement between the CPU and the cooler. Applying it correctly helps keep efficient heat dissipation.

2. Case Fans: These work in combination with your cooler to improve airflow. More fans can improve cooling, but be mindful of noise levels and case space.

Choosing the Right Cooling System:

- For most gaming PCs, air cooling is fine, especially if you're not overclocking.
- If you plan on overclocking your CPU or GPU, or if you want a quieter PC with a cleaner look, consider a liquid cooling option.
- Always make sure your case supports the cooling solution you choose, especially when it comes to radiator space in liquid cooling setups.

Peripheral Devices (Mouse, Keyboard, Monitor, etc.)

While the core components of your PC provide the performance, peripheral devices improve your gaming experience. These devices—such as your mouse, keyboard, and monitor—are your direct interaction with the game. Choosing the right peripherals can make a major difference in gameplay, ease, and immersion.

Mouse:

A gaming mouse is intended to provide precision, speed, and comfort. It's one of the most critical tools for gaming, especially for first-person shooters (FPS) and real-time strategy (RTS) games. A high-quality mouse can make the difference between a smooth, enjoyable game experience and a frustrating one.

Key Features to Look For:

1. DPI (Dots Per Inch): This measures the sharpness of the mouse. Higher DPI means quicker moves on-screen. Look for a mouse that allows you to change DPI for different games or playstyles.

 2. Ergonomics: A comfortable mouse can avoid strain during long gaming sessions. Consider the shape, grip style (claw, palm, fingertip), and general feel.

3. Polling Rate: This refers to how often the mouse sends its position to the PC. Higher polling rates (e.g., 1000Hz) provide smoother and more rapid tracking.

Keyboard:

A gaming keyboard is meant to provide better responsiveness and comfort than a standard keyboard. Features like mechanical switches and customizable keycaps offer improved control and durability for gamers.

Key Features to Look For:

1. Mechanical vs. Membrane: Mechanical keyboards provide a tactile feedback and quicker reaction, making them the preferred choice for gaming. Membrane keyboards are quieter and more cheap but can feel less responsive.

2. Key Rollover and Anti-Ghosting: These features ensure that multiple key presses are registered properly. This is particularly important in fast-paced games where you might be hitting multiple keys simultaneously.

3. Customization: Many gaming keyboards allow you to program keys for macros or adjust the lighting, which can give you a more personalized gaming experience.

Monitor:

Your monitor is where you experience the game, so it's critical to choose one that offers clear, vibrant visuals and high refresh rates to match your gaming style.

Key Features to Look For:

1. **Resolution:** Higher resolutions provide sharper pictures. A 1080p resolution is common for most games, but if you have a powerful GPU, you might try 1440p (QHD) or 4K for ultra-high definition.

2. **Refresh Rate:** The refresh rate (measured in Hz) shows how often the image on your screen is refreshed per second. A higher refresh rate (e.g.,

144Hz or 240Hz) leads to smoother visuals, which is especially important for competitive games.

3. Response Time: Measured in milliseconds (ms), this refers to how quickly a pixel changes color. A lower response time (e.g., 1ms) minimizes motion blur and ghosting, which is important for fast-moving action games.

4. G-Sync / Free Sync: These technologies synchronize your monitor's refresh rate with your GPU to eliminate screen tearing and stuttering, providing a smoother game experience.

Other Essential Peripherals:

1. Headset: A good gaming headset not only provides immersive sound but also allows you to communicate with other players. Look for a headset with noise-canceling features and a quality microphone for clear conversation.

2. Gamepad / Joystick: For games that require more precise or different controls, such as racing or fighting games, a gamepad or joystick can provide a better experience than a mouse and computer.

3. Mouse Pad: A big, smooth mouse pad can improve tracking accuracy, especially with high-DPI mice. Some game mouse pads even come with built-in RGB lighting.

By choosing the right cooling system and peripherals, you can greatly enhance both the performance and the comfort of your gaming experience. Whether you're building a powerful, high-performance rig or looking to fine-tune your gaming setup, these components are important for getting the most out of your system.

Chapter 3: Assembling Your Gaming PC (Step-by-Step)

Building your own game PC can be a satisfying and fulfilling experience. While the process may seem complex at first, taking it step by step will ensure you assemble your components properly and safely. In this part, we'll guide you through each phase of the assembly, making sure you understand every step along the way.

Preparing Your Workspace and Tools

Before diving into the build, setting up a proper workspace is important. A clean, well-lit, and organized area helps avoid mistakes and keeps parts safe from damage. Here's what you'll need:

Tools Required:

1. Phillips-head screwdriver: The most widely used tool in PC assembly, needed for screwing in the

motherboard, power supply, and other components.

2. Anti-static wrist strap: This stops static electricity from damaging your components. Attach it to a grounded item (like a metal part of your case) while working.

3. Cable ties/Velcro straps: For managing wires and keeping your build neat.

4. Thermal paste (if not pre-applied): Used when fitting the CPU cooler to ensure good heat transfer between the CPU and cooler.

Setting Up the Workspace:

1. Clean area: Use a large, clean, flat area free of dust or debris. Ideally, work on a non-static surface, like a hard table, not a carpet.

2. Organize Components: Lay out all the components neatly, making sure everything you need is easily available. Check your parts list to ensure you have everything.

3. Good Lighting: Proper lighting helps you see small joints and screws clearly, making assembly easier and reducing mistakes.

Installing the CPU, RAM, and Cooler

Now that your workspace is ready, it's time to start loading the internal components. The CPU, RAM, and cooler are some of the first parts to add.

1. Installing the CPU:

1. Open the CPU Socket: On your motherboard, find the CPU socket and lift the retention bar. This reveals the socket where the CPU will sit.

2. line the CPU: Carefully remove the CPU from its packaging and line it with the socket. There will be a small triangle or marking on the CPU and motherboard to help guide the position.

3. Install the CPU: Gently put the CPU into the socket without applying force. Once it's in place, lower the retention arm to seal it.

2. Installing the RAM:

1. Locate the RAM Slots: On the motherboard, there will be slots especially for RAM. These are generally labeled and color-coded for optimal performance.

2. Install the RAM: Open the clips on either side of the RAM space. Line up the holes on the RAM stick with the slot, and firmly press down until the clips click into place.

3. Installing the Cooler:

1. add Thermal Paste: If your CPU cooler doesn't come with pre-applied thermal paste, add a small, pea-sized amount of thermal paste to the center of the CPU.

2. Attach the Cooler: Carefully put the cooler over the CPU, aligning it with the mounting holes. Once in place, lock the cooler by screwing it into the motherboard. Ensure that it's tightly attached, but don't overtighten.

Installing the Motherboard into the Case

With the CPU, RAM, and cooler installed, it's time to place the motherboard into the case.

1. Install Standoffs in the Case: Standoffs are small metal screws that lift the motherboard off the case, avoiding short circuits. Install these in the case according to the motherboard's fixing holes.

2. Align the Motherboard: Line up the I/O ports (the ports for USB, Ethernet, etc.) with the back of the box. Gently lower the motherboard into the case, ensuring that it sits on the standoffs.

3. Screw in the Motherboard: Once in place, secure the motherboard by putting it into the standoffs. Make sure it's snug but not too tight.

Installing the GPU and Storage

With the motherboard fixed, we'll move on to installing the GPU (Graphics Processing Unit) and storage devices.

1. Installing the GPU:

1. Locate the PCIe Slot: On the motherboard, find the PCIe x16 slot where the GPU will be placed. This spot is usually the longest one.

2. Insert the GPU: Gently match the GPU's PCIe connector with the slot. Firmly press down until the card clicks into place.

3. Secure the GPU: Use the screws on the back of the case to secure the GPU to the case. This will keep the card from shifting during use.

2. Installing the Storage (SSD or HDD):

1. Mount the Storage Device: Depending on whether you're installing an SSD or HDD, use the proper mounting bracket or bay in your case. SSDs usually go in 2.5-inch bays, while HDDs are generally mounted in 3.5-inch bays.

2. Secure the Drive: For SSDs, simply screw them into place in the 2.5-inch bracket. For HDDs, mount them securely using screws or a tool-less mounting method.

3. Connect the Storage: Use the SATA connection to connect the SSD/HDD to the motherboard. Then, connect the power cord from the PSU to the drive.

Connecting Power Cables and Peripherals

Next, it's time to connect the power source and peripherals.

1. Connecting Power Supply:

1. Install the PSU: Slide the power supply into the bottom or top compartment of your case, based on the design. Secure it with screws.

2. Connect the 24-pin Power Cable: This cable is the main power port for your motherboard. Plug it into the motherboard's 24-pin power port.

3. Connect the CPU Power wire: This 4-pin or 8-pin wire powers the CPU. Plug it into the appropriate socket near the CPU.

4. Connect GPU Power: If your GPU needs power (which most modern GPUs do), connect the 6-pin or 8-pin power cables from the PSU to the GPU.

2. Connecting Peripherals:

1. Mouse and Keyboard: Plug your mouse and keyboard into the USB ports on the computer or through a USB hub if you have one.

2. Monitor: Use the proper cable (HDMI, DisplayPort, etc.) to connect your monitor to the

GPU. If you're using embedded graphics, plug it into the motherboard's video-out port.

Finalizing the Setup

At this point, your gaming PC is nearly ready to turn on! There are a few final checks and steps to ensure everything is properly connected and safe.

1. Cable Management: Use cable ties or Velcro straps to tidy up your cords. This helps with airflow and keeps the body of your case looking clean.

2. Double-Check Connections: Go over each connection again—ensure the power cords, data cables, and peripheral connections are properly seated.

3. Test Boot: Connect your PC to a monitor, plug in the power line, and press the power button. If everything is connected properly, the machine should start. You should see the motherboard logo or BIOS screen on the computer. If the system doesn't boot, double-check the connections, and make sure the PSU is turned on.

Congratulations! You've successfully built your gaming PC. From here, you can move on to downloading the operating system, drivers, and games. But before diving into gaming, remember to maintain your system, watch temperatures, and periodically clean out dust to keep your build running smoothly for years to come.

Chapter 4: Choosing the Right Operating System for Gaming

The operating system (OS) you choose for your gaming PC is one of the most important choices you'll make. It influences everything from game compatibility to performance optimization. While most gaming PCs run Windows, Linux is also a choice for more advanced users.

In this chapter, we'll compare Windows and Linux, provide a detailed guide to setting up and optimizing Windows for gaming, and talk how to install essential drivers and software for the best gaming experience.

Windows vs. Linux for Gaming

When it comes to games, Windows has been the go-to OS for decades. It is by far the most popular choice due to its compatibility with nearly all gaming gear, software, and game titles. Most games are created with Windows in mind, and a wide range of tools and services are available to enhance the gaming experience.

Why Choose Windows?

1. Game Compatibility: Windows supports the biggest library of games, from AAA titles to indie games.

2. Driver Support: Almost all hardware makers release drivers and software optimized for Windows.

3. Performance: Windows is well-optimized for gaming, with regular updates and support for DirectX, which greatly boosts gaming performance.

Why Consider Linux?

While Linux is a great operating system for developers and power users, it is not usually the best choice for gaming, especially if you want an easy and seamless experience. However, with tools like Steam's Proton, Linux has become more gaming-friendly in recent years.

Advantages of Linux:

1. Free and Open-Source: Linux is completely free, unlike Windows, which needs a paid license.

2. Lightweight: Linux distributions are often less resource-intensive than Windows, meaning they can offer better performance for certain jobs.

3. Customization: Linux allows for full customization of the system and environment.

Limitations of Linux for Gaming:

1. Limited Game Support: Not all games are available for Linux. While many big games can be run through Proton or Wine, some titles still do not work well or are unsupported.

2. Driver and Software Issues: Some hardware, especially peripherals, may have restricted or no support in Linux.

Conclusion: For most gamers, Windows is the clear choice due to its wide compatibility with games, hardware, and gaming-related software. If you are an experienced user who likes tinkering with systems and prioritizing open-source software, Linux can be a viable option, but you may face limitations with game compatibility and performance.

Setting Up and Optimizing Windows for Gaming

Once you've chosen Windows as your operating system, the next step is to install it and optimize it for games. Here's how to get started:

1. Installing Windows:

Start by getting the latest version of Windows from the official Microsoft website. You'll need a USB drive (at least 8 GB in size) to make a bootable installation drive using Windows Media Creation Tool.

- Insert the USB drive into your game PC, restart it, and boot from the USB. Follow the on-screen steps to install Windows on your primary drive (usually an SSD for faster boot times and game loading).

2. Optimizing Windows Settings for Gaming:

After installation, it's important to tweak some settings to ensure the OS is running at peak performance:

1. **Disable Unnecessary Startup Programs:** Many applications set themselves to start immediately when Windows boots. Disable these from Task Manager to lower resource consumption.

2. **Power Settings:** Go to Control Panel > Power Options, and select the High-Performance power plan to ensure your CPU and GPU aren't throttled when gaming.

3. **Disable graphic Effects:** Windows includes graphic effects that can take up system resources. Go to System Properties >

Advanced System Settings and adjust for better performance.

3. Enabling Game Mode:

Windows 10 and later come with a Game Mode feature, which prioritizes gaming speed by limiting background processes. You can activate Game Mode in Settings > Gaming > Game Mode.

Installing Essential Drivers and Software

Once Windows is set up, it's important to install the necessary drivers and software to ensure your game PC runs smoothly.

1. Graphics Card Driver (GPU):

1. **The GPU driver** is one of the most important drivers for gaming performance. Download the latest drivers straight from the NVIDIA or AMD website (depending on your GPU).

2. Make sure to select the right model and operating system version to ensure compatibility. Running outdated drivers can cause speed issues or crashes in games.

2. Motherboard and Chipset Drivers:

Installing the **chipset drivers** from your motherboard manufacturer ensures that your CPU, RAM, and other components work at their best. These drivers help improve system stability and speed.

3. Peripheral Drivers:

If you have specialized game peripherals such as a gaming mouse, keyboard, or gaming headset, download the necessary software from the manufacturer's website. These drivers often come with customization tools, such as setting up key macros, RGB lights, and DPI profiles.

4. Game-Related Software:

1. **Steam** is the most popular platform for buying and playing games, so make sure you have it installed. Steam also offers useful features like cloud saving, game streaming, and performance monitoring.
2. Other platforms like **Epic Games Store**, Origin, or GOG Galaxy may also be necessary based on where your games are purchased.

Keeping the OS Updated for Maximum Performance

To ensure your gaming PC stays in top condition, you must keep your operating system updated. Regular updates provide important security patches, improve system stability, and sometimes even enhance gaming performance.

1. Windows Updates:

1. Windows usually handles updates automatically. However, it's important to ensure that updates are regularly loaded. You can check for changes manually by going to Settings > Update & Security > Windows Update.

2. Occasionally, **updates** can cause system problems or game crashes. If this happens,

you may want to delay or remove certain updates until they are patched by Microsoft.

2. Driver Updates:

1. Graphics drivers should be updated frequently to take advantage of speed optimizations and bug fixes for newly released games. Many GPU makers like NVIDIA and AMD offer tools that automatically check for and install updates.

2. Windows Update may not always update every hardware driver, so you should occasionally visit the manufacturer's website for changes, especially for peripherals like your sound card or networking devices.

3. System Cleanup and Disk Optimization:

1. Over time, temporary files, cached data, and other useless system files can slow down your PC. Use tools like Disk Cleanup or CCleaner to remove junk files.
2. For SSD users, Windows will automatically handle defragmentation, but if you're using an HDD, you can manually defrag your drives via Defragment and Optimize Drives in Windows.

4. Performance Monitoring:

Use tools like Task Manager or third-party apps like MSI Afterburner to monitor system resources such as CPU, GPU, RAM, and disk usage. This can help you spot bottlenecks or areas that might require further optimization.

By carefully picking the right operating system, installing the essential software and drivers, and keeping your system updated, you'll ensure that your gaming PC offers the best performance for your games. The right setup not only improves your game experience but also ensures stability and longevity for your system.

Chapter 5: Gaming Accessories and Peripherals

While the core components of your gaming PC determine your system's performance, the right gaming accessories and peripherals can enhance your total gaming experience. Whether you're looking for a high-quality game monitor, a responsive keyboard and mouse, or immersive audio equipment, choosing the right gear is key to getting the most out of your setup.

In this chapter, we'll walk through the essential accessories for your gaming PC, giving detailed advice on how to choose and set them up for maximum comfort and performance.

Choosing the Best Gaming Monitor

The monitor is probably one of the most important peripherals when it comes to gaming. It's where you'll be spending the most time, so having the right display is important to your gaming experience. When choosing a gaming monitor, there are several factors to consider that can greatly impact how your games look and perform.

Key Factors to Consider:

1. Resolution: The higher the resolution, the sharper and more detailed the picture will be.

Common gaming settings include:

- 1080p (Full HD): A good choice for budget builds or casual players.
- 1440p (Quad HD): Offers a sharper picture without demanding as much power as 4K.
- 4K (Ultra HD): Best for high-end gaming setups, offering stunning visuals but needs a powerful GPU.

2. Refresh Rate: The refresh rate refers to how many times the monitor updates the picture per second, measured in Hz. A faster refresh rate results in smoother gameplay, especially for fast-paced games like FPS (First-Person Shooters).

Common restart rates include:

- 60Hz: Standard, good for general use.
- 120Hz/144Hz: Great for most gamers, giving smooth and fluid visuals.
- 240Hz: Best for competitive gamers who expect ultra-smooth gameplay and minimal motion blur.

• **Response Time:** Measured in milliseconds (ms), response time shows how quickly a pixel changes color. Lower response times are important for fast-moving games like shooters, where quick reactions are essential. Aim for 1ms to 3ms for competitive games.

• **G-Sync and FreeSync:** These technologies help remove screen tearing by syncing the monitor's refresh rate with the GPU's frame rate, creating smoother visuals. G-Sync is for NVIDIA

GPUs, while FreeSync is for AMD GPUs. Choose the one that fits your GPU to improve the gaming experience.

Keyboards and Mice: Mechanical vs. Membrane

Your keyboard and mouse are your main input devices, and the type you choose can significantly impact your game performance and comfort.

Keyboards:

Mechanical Keyboards: Known for their tactile feedback and durability, mechanical keyboards are the go-to choice for serious players. They use individual switches under each key, giving a more responsive feel and faster keypress registration.

Mechanical keyboards come in different switch types, including:

- Linear (Red, Black): Quiet and smooth, great for fast-paced games.
- Tactile (Brown, Clear): Provide a slight bump when the key is pressed, giving feedback without being too loud.
- Clicky (Blue, Green): Loud and clicky, great for typists but can be distracting in shared settings.

Membrane Keyboards: These are usually quieter and less expensive, but they lack the same tactile feel and durability of mechanical keyboards. Membrane keyboards are softer to press and quieter, making them a good choice if you're on a budget or if you need something more discreet.

Mice

- ## **Wired vs. Wireless:**

While wired mice offer a more stable and responsive link with no latency, wireless mice have become highly efficient, offering freedom of movement and near-zero latency. A wireless mouse with low latency is great for gaming.

- DPI (Dots Per Inch): DPI tracks the sensitivity of the mouse. Higher DPI means more sensitivity, allowing you to make exact movements quickly.

- Gaming mice often come with adjustable DPI settings to allow you to tailor the sensitivity based on your game or taste. For FPS games, a high DPI (2000–16000) is ideal for rapid movements, while a lower DPI (800–1600) is often better for RTS or MOBA games where accuracy is key.

- Ergonomics: Comfort matters for long game sessions. Look for a mouse that fits your hand well. An ergonomic design can help avoid wrist strain, especially if you game for hours.

Gaming Headsets: Audio Quality and Comfort A gaming headset provides immersive audio and communication with your team, making it an essential accessory for most players. When choosing a gaming headset, consider both audio quality and comfort, as both can greatly impact your gaming experience.

Key Factors to Consider:

1. Sound Quality: Look for a headset that offers clear, rich sound with good bass. Surround sound (such as 7.1 surround) can help you better hear in-game audio cues, like footsteps or faraway gunfire, giving you a competitive edge in FPS games.

2. Microphone Quality: A good microphone is important for communicating with teammates. Look for a headset with a noise-canceling microphone that can filter out background noise and ensure your message is clear.

3. Comfort: Gaming sessions can last for hours, so comfort is key. Look for a headset with padded ear cups and an adjustable headband to ensure a snug but comfy fit. Lightweight designs reduce pressure on your head and ears, while soft memory foam can help with long-term comfort.

4. Wired vs. Wireless: Wired headsets offer no delay and are often cheaper, but wireless headsets provide greater freedom of movement. Choose based on whether you value mobility or want the best possible sound and reliability.

Game Controllers and Additional Gear

While keyboard and mouse setups are chosen for many gamers, certain genres benefit from a game controller or extra gaming gear, like a gaming chair or RGB lighting for a personalized experience.

- **Game Controllers:**

For racing, fighting, or platformer games, a controller may feel more natural and provide better control. Popular controllers include: o Xbox Wireless Controller: Known for its ergonomic design and smooth compatibility with Windows PCs.

- PlayStation DualSense Controller: Offers advanced features like adaptive triggers and haptic feedback (for those with a PlayStation system).
- Third-party Controllers: Companies like Logitech and Razer offer high-quality controllers with adjustable buttons and ergonomic features.
- Additional Gear: Consider investing in gaming chairs made for long hours of gameplay with ergonomic support, or RGB lighting to enhance the aesthetics of your gaming setup.

Setting Up and Configuring Your Accessories

Once you've chosen your accessories, it's time to set them up and configure them to fit your needs. Monitor Setup: Place your monitor at eye level for best comfort. Adjust the brightness and contrast to your liking, and set the correct resolution and refresh rate in your graphics settings to match your GPU's powers.

- **Keyboard and Mouse Configuration:**

Connect your keyboard and mouse, and if you're using a mechanical keyboard, consider customizing keybinds using tools like Razer Synapse or Logitech G HUB. For mice, adjust the DPI settings through the specialized software to match your gaming style.

- **Headset Setup:**

Plug in or connect your headset and change audio settings in your system's sound settings. Ensure the microphone is clear and set the volume levels to prevent hearing damage during long game sessions.

- Controller Configuration:

If you're using a controller, install the necessary drivers (usually automatic on Windows) and calibrate it through Steam Big Picture Mode or your game's settings to ensure maximum response.

This chapter on gaming accessories and peripherals will give you the tools you need to optimize your gaming setup for both speed and comfort. The right accessories not only improve gameplay but also ensure that your gaming experience is immersive, enjoyable, and tailored to your tastes.

Chapter 6: Overclocking Your Gaming PC

Overclocking your gaming PC is a powerful way to increase speed without upgrading your hardware. It includes pushing your CPU, GPU, or RAM to run faster than the default settings provided by the manufacturer. Although it can significantly improve your gaming experience, it takes a clear understanding of the risks and how to manage them.

This chapter will cover everything you need to know about overclocking, from understanding its benefits and risks to running stability tests and monitoring your system.

What is Overclocking and Why Do It?

Overclocking refers to the process of running a component—most commonly the CPU or GPU—at a faster speed than it was originally meant to run. Each processor has a default clock speed, which is the rate at which it completes orders. By increasing the clock speed, you can make the processor finish tasks faster, giving you an overall boost in performance.

Why Overclock?

Overclocking can give your gaming experience a noticeable boost, especially in CPU-bound games or jobs like simulations, real-time strategy (RTS) games, and other demanding applications. It can also help squeeze out more speed from your GPU for better frame rates in graphically intense games.

However, the gains aren't always dramatic, and overclocking takes a balanced approach to avoid damaging your hardware. The improvement you see will depend on the individual components you are overclocking and how well they respond to the changes.

Understanding CPU and GPU Overclocking

- **CPU Overclocking**

The CPU is the brain of your PC, handling calculations and executing jobs. By increasing its clock speed (measured in GHz), you can improve the performance of CPU-intensive apps like physics calculations, AI, and other in-game processes. Modern CPUs also come with multiple cores, so overclocking can improve the overall performance of the system, especially in multi-threaded applications.

o How to Overclock a CPU:

Overclocking the CPU can usually be done through the BIOS/UEFI settings of your computer. This includes adjusting the base clock (BCLK) or the multiplier to increase the CPU's clock speed. You can also change the voltage to provide the necessary power for stable overclocking.

o Risks of CPU Overclocking:

Pushing the CPU too far without proper cooling can lead to overheating, instability, and possible damage. A stable overclock needs careful fine-tuning, proper cooling, and stress testing to ensure reliability.

- **GPU Overclocking**

GPU overclocking is often easier than CPU overclocking because many GPUs come with built-in overclocking software, such as NVIDIA's Afterburner or AMD's Radeon Software. By raising the GPU's clock speed, you can improve performance in graphics-heavy games, resulting in smoother frame rates and better resolution at higher settings.

o How to Overclock a GPU:

Use software tools like MSI Afterburner, which allows you to change the GPU's core clock, memory clock, and voltage. Most of the adjustments are simple sliders, and you can increase each number gradually, testing stability as you go.

- Risks of GPU Overclocking:

Just like with the CPU, overclocking the GPU too aggressively without proper cooling can result in overheating and instability. Monitoring temperatures is key, and it's always a good idea to test your changes carefully with stress tests or benchmark programs.

Tools and Software for Overclocking

To safely boost your components, you'll need a few tools and utilities:

- **For CPU Overclocking:**

BIOS/UEFI Settings: Most motherboards allow overclocking straight through the BIOS or UEFI firmware interface. From here, you can change multipliers, voltage settings, and base clock speeds.

Intel Extreme Tuning Utility (XTU) or AMD Ryzen Master: These tools allow you to fine-tune your CPU's clock speeds and voltages within the operating system, making it easier to test changes without restarting into the BIOS.

- **For GPU Overclocking:**

MSI Afterburner: One of the most popular tools for overclocking GPUs, MSI Afterburner allows you to change core clock, memory clock, and fan speeds. It also offers real-time monitoring and stress testing features.

EVGA Precision X1: Another great tool for NVIDIA cards, giving detailed controls over the GPU's performance, including fan curves and voltage adjustments.

- **For Monitoring:**

HWMonitor or Core Temp: These tools help you monitor the temperatures, voltage, and usage of different components. It's important to keep track of the temperatures while overclocking to ensure your system doesn't overheat.

FurMark or 3DMark: Stress testing tools to test GPU reliability under load. 3DMark is particularly useful for benchmarking your system's speed before and after overclocking.

Tips for Safe Overclocking

Overclocking can be exciting, but it's important to do it safely to avoid damaging your components.

Here are some key tips to follow:

- Increase Gradually:

Don't make big jumps in clock speeds. Increase in small increments, normally 50 MHz at a time for CPUs and 10-20 MHz for GPUs, and test for stability at each stage.

- Monitor Temperatures:

Always keep an eye on the temperatures of your CPU and GPU. You want to keep the temperature below 85°C for the CPU and under 80°C for the GPU to avoid thermal slowdown or long-term damage.

- Stress Test After Every Change:

Use stress-testing tools like Prime95 for CPUs and FurMark for GPUs to verify that your overclock is stable. Run the stress test for at least 30 minutes to check if your system crashes or if any mistakes occur.

- Adjust Voltages Carefully:

If your machine becomes unstable after overclocking, you may need to increase the voltage slightly. But don't overdo it—increasing voltage too much can generate excessive heat and possibly damage the component.

• Use Quality Cooling Solutions:

If you're serious about boosting, invest in quality cooling. Air coolers with bigger heatsinks or AIO liquid cooling systems will provide better thermal performance, allowing you to push your components further.

Stability Testing and Monitoring Overclocked Systems

After making your adjustments, it's important to test your system for stability. Overclocking changes the way your system works, and instability is a common issue.

• **Stress Testing:** Stress testing is the process of pushing your system to its limits to ensure that the overclocked components can handle the load without crashing or causing errors. Use tools like Prime95 (for CPU), AIDA64, and FurMark (for GPU) to stress test the machine.

• **Monitoring Software:** Tools like HWMonitor and MSI Afterburner give you real-time views into the temperatures, voltages, and frequencies of your components, so you can ensure that your overclock is stable and not causing overheating or system crashes.

Overclocking is a powerful way to improve the performance of your gaming PC, but it requires knowledge and caution. By following the proper steps, using the right tools, and checking stability carefully, you can safely overclock your CPU and GPU to boost your gaming experience.

Remember, the goal is to achieve a balance between performance and stability, so always monitor your system and make gradual changes.

With the right method, overclocking can unlock extra power, giving your gaming PC the edge it needs to run the latest games smoothly.

Chapter 7: Maintenance, Testing, and Fault Finding

After building and overclocking your gaming PC, it's important to maintain it to ensure that it continues to perform at its best. Regular maintenance, testing, and the ability to troubleshoot problems can greatly extend the lifespan of your system and avoid performance drops or hardware failures.

In this chapter, we'll discuss the key practices to keep your gaming PC running smoothly, how to run performance tests, and how to spot and fix common problems.

Keeping Your Gaming PC Clean and Dust-Free

One of the most important aspects of maintaining your gaming PC is ensuring that it stays clean and free from dust. Dust buildup can block airflow, making your cooling system less effective, and it can also cause components to boil. This not only leads to reduced speed but also shortens the lifespan of your hardware.

How to Keep Your PC Clean:

• **Positioning:** Place your PC in a location that's generally dust-free and away from vents or fans that might blow dust into your case.

• **Dust Filters:** Install dust filters on intake and exit fans. These screens prevent dust from entering your case and can be cleaned regularly.

- **Regular Cleaning:** Use a can of compressed air to blow out dust from the case, especially around the CPU, GPU, and power supply. Be gentle when cleaning delicate components. Hold fans in place to avoid spinning them while cleaning.

- **Avoid Liquids:** When cleaning the exterior, use a soft, dry cloth to wipe down surfaces. Avoid using liquids or cleaners that can damage gadgets.

Routine Maintenance to Ensure Longevity

Just as with any high-performance machine, routine maintenance is important to keep your gaming PC running smoothly over time. Here's what you should do to keep peak performance:

1. Monitor temps:

- Regularly check the temps of your CPU, GPU, and other components. High temperatures can lead to throttling or permanent harm.

- Use tools like HWMonitor, Core Temp, or MSI Afterburner to track temperatures in real time. If temperatures are too high, try adding more cooling or improving airflow within your case.

2. Update Software and Drivers:

- Keep your drivers up-to-date, especially for the GPU. Manufacturers often release driver updates that improve game performance and fix bugs.

- Windows updates and security patches should be installed regularly to ensure your system is running optimally and safely.

3. Reapply Thermal Paste:

- Over time, thermal paste on your CPU or GPU can weaken. It's a good idea to replace it every 1-2 years for better cooling performance.

4. Check for Wear and Tear:

- Inspect cables for fraying or damage, and ensure that there are no loose links inside your PC.

- Pay attention to the condition of your power supply unit (PSU) and consider replacing it if it starts showing signs of failure, such as loud fan noise or intermittent power problems.

Running Benchmarks to Test Performance

Benchmarking is a method used to evaluate the performance of your PC by running tests that simulate different workloads. For gamers, benchmarks can help you determine if your system is working at its full potential and if overclocking has had the desired effect.

Common Benchmarking Tools:

• **3DMark:** This is one of the most famous tools for benchmarking your gaming PC. It tests your system's performance with different graphical workloads and gives you a performance number to compare with other systems.

• **Unigine Heaven/Valley:** These are great tools for testing the speed of your GPU. They run demanding graphical scenarios that stress your GPU and help identify potential problems.

• **Cinebench:** This is a CPU-focused measure that stresses the processor to test its multi-core and single-core performance. It's great for testing the effect of overclocking your CPU.

What to Look For:

• **Frame Rates:** In games, aim for 60 FPS (frames per second) as a standard for smooth gameplay. Higher FPS (120 FPS or more) is ideal for fast-paced games, especially with high-refresh-rate TVs.

• **Stability:** Consistent frame rates and stable performance during benchmarks suggest that your system is running smoothly.

• **Temperature and Power Usage**: Monitoring these factors during a benchmark will help you assess whether your cooling system is adequate and if your components are using power effectively.

Troubleshooting Common Gaming PC Issues

Even with the best components, your gaming PC may face issues over time. Knowing how to troubleshoot and identify problems is key to getting your system back up and running. Common Issues and How to Fix Them:

1. PC Won't Boot:

- o **Check Power Supply:** Ensure the PSU is linked properly. Verify if the PSU switch is on and that all power cables are safe.
- o **RAM Issues:** Reseat your RAM sticks. Try starting with one stick of RAM to check if one is faulty.
- o **Motherboard Lights or Beeps:** Check the motherboard manual for diagnostic LEDs or beep codes to spot hardware issues.

2. Slow Performance or Frame Drops:

- **Overheating:** If your machine is overheating, it will throttle performance. Check temperatures and better airflow or cooling if needed.

- **Driver Issues:** Outdated or incompatible drivers can lead to bad performance. Ensure all your drivers, especially the GPU, are up-to-date.

- **Background Processes:** Use the Task Manager (Ctrl + Shift + Esc) to close unnecessary apps running in the background that may consume system resources.

3. Artifacts or Visual Glitches in Games:

- GPU Overclocking Issues: If you've boosted your GPU, it may be unstable. Try lowering the overclock or resetting to normal settings.

o Graphics Drivers: Make sure your GPU drivers are updated, as bugs in older drivers can cause visual glitches.

Fault-Finding: Diagnosing Hardware Problems

Diagnosing hardware problems can be tricky, but it's important to know how to pinpoint the source of a problem. Here's how to approach identifying hardware-related issues:

1. Isolate the Problem:

• **Power Issues:** If your system isn't turning on, start by checking the PSU, cables, and power button connections.

• **Screen or Display Issues**: If you're having problems with your monitor (like no signal), check the GPU connection, monitor wire, and input settings.

- **Unusual Noises:** If your PC is making strange sounds, it could be a failed fan, PSU, or hard drive. Run diagnostic tests to check the health of these components.

2. Test Individual Components:

- **RAM:** Run MemTest86 to check for bad memory.

- **Hard Drive/SSD:** Use tools like Crystal Disk Info to check the health of your hard drives.

- **GPU and CPU:** Run stress tests (like Fur Mark for GPUs and Prime95 for CPUs) to see if any component is hot or crashing under load.

3. Check for Software Conflicts:

• Sometimes, the problem may not be with the hardware but with software. Conflicts between drivers or running too many apps can cause instability. Clean up your system, clear bloatware, and reinstall drivers if necessary.

Maintaining, testing, and troubleshooting your gaming PC are important parts of keeping it running at peak performance. Regular cleaning, running benchmarks, and keeping your system updated are all crucial for avoiding problems. If problems do arise, learning how to diagnose and fix them can save you time and prevent costly repairs.

By following the steps outlined in this chapter, you can ensure that your gaming PC stays reliable, powerful, and ready for anything.

Chapter 8: Updates for Your Gaming PC

The world of gaming technology moves quickly, and keeping your system updated is important to ensure your gaming PC remains relevant and capable of handling new titles and software.

Regular changes to drivers, software, and hardware upgrades will help your PC stay in top shape. In this chapter, we'll cover how to keep your system updated, how to prepare it for future games, and how to install your chosen games efficiently.

Keeping Drivers and Software Updated

Your gaming PC's drivers are critical for ensuring that your hardware functions properly with your operating system and gaming software. The GPU, CPU, motherboard, and peripherals all rely on drivers to connect effectively with the rest of your system. Keeping these drivers updated will ensure maximum speed, compatibility, and stability.

Why It's Important:

• **GPU Drivers:** Video card manufacturers like NVIDIA and AMD regularly release driver updates to fix bugs, improve speed, and ensure compatibility with the latest games. Updating your GPU drivers ensures that you're getting the best possible performance from your graphics card, often improving frame rates and visual quality in new games.

• **CPU and Motherboard Drivers:** While these don't get as many updates as GPU drivers, it's still essential to keep your CPU and motherboard drivers up-to-date for system stability, especially with firmware updates that can improve compatibility with new games or software.

• **devices:** Gaming devices like mice, keyboards, and headsets may also have firmware or driver changes. These updates can increase their usefulness, fix known issues, and improve performance.

How to Update:

• **Windows Update:** Windows has a built-in feature to check for updates to important drivers automatically.

- **Manufacturer Websites:** For graphics card drivers, visit NVIDIA, AMD, or your card's maker page to download the latest drivers.

- **Third-Party Tools:** Tools like Driver Booster can help you keep all of your drivers updated with minimal work.

Regularly checking for updates ensures that your gaming PC is always running best and is prepared for any game or software release.

Upgrading Your Hardware for Future Games

Gaming hardware has a limited lifespan, and as new, more demanding titles are released, you may need to upgrade specific components to keep up with the growing demands. While overclocking and software optimizations can help stretch the life of your current hardware, there will inevitably come a time when a hardware upgrade is necessary to play future games at their best.

Key Components to Consider for Future Proofing:

• **GPU (Graphics Card):** The GPU is the most important part of your machine when it comes to gaming performance. As game graphics develop and become more complex, a powerful GPU is crucial for running newer titles smoothly. If you're currently using an older card, upgrading to a more powerful one (e.g., from an NVIDIA RTX 30 series to a 40 series) will provide a large boost in frame rates and visual quality.

• **CPU:** While the CPU isn't always the bottleneck in gaming performance (that role usually belongs to the GPU), certain games, especially open-world or simulation games, demand a lot from the CPU. Upgrading to a faster CPU can make a visible difference in gameplay.

• **RAM:** Most modern games run easily with 16GB of RAM, but as games become more resource-intensive, 32GB or more may be necessary. Increasing your RAM will help your system run more quickly during multitasking and when playing demanding games.

• **Storage:** As games grow in size, having an SSD (Solid State Drive) is important for faster loading times. An NVMe SSD is much faster than a standard SATA SSD and is highly suggested for future-proofing.

How to Upgrade:

• Research Compatibility: Make sure that the new components are compatible with your current motherboard and case. Some high-end GPUs, for example, require bigger cases or more power.

• **Install Drivers:** After upgrading components like the GPU or CPU, ensure that the right drivers are installed for optimal performance. By upgrading key components as your needs grow, your gaming PC can continue to work at a high level for years to come.

Best Practices for Preventing Obsolescence

One of the challenges of building a gaming PC is ensuring that it doesn't become obsolete too fast. As games evolve, the hardware needed to run them efficiently also changes. However, by following some best practices, you can keep your gaming rig useful for a longer time.

Best Practices:

• **Balanced Build:** When building your PC, focus on having a balanced setup. Don't skimp on important components like the CPU, GPU, or power supply. A well-balanced build with good-quality parts will ensure you don't hit bottlenecks that limit your upgrade options in the future.

• **Monitor Gaming Trends:** Pay attention to the games that are trending or being created in the coming years. If you're into AAA games that focus on high-end graphics, consider future-proofing by getting a more powerful GPU and a faster CPU.

• **Upgrade Gradually:** Instead of upgrading all your components at once, focus on upgrading the parts that will make the most effect. For example, upgrading the GPU first will give the most noticeable improvement in your gaming experience. Afterward, you can focus on improving the CPU or adding more RAM.

By keeping your system balanced and upgrading in stages, you can avoid making your game rig obsolete too soon.

Ensuring the System Can Handle New Games

New games are often more demanding than previous ones, especially with improvements in graphics, physics, and artificial intelligence. To ensure your system can handle the latest games, it's important to monitor your hardware's performance regularly and change accordingly.

How to Ensure Performance:

• **System Requirements:** Always check the minimum and suggested system requirements for new games. This can help you determine if your present build is capable of running the game or if it needs an upgrade.

• **Benchmarking Tools:** Use benchmarking software to test how your system works with new games. Tools like 3DMark or Unigine Heaven can give you a performance number that you can compare with other systems to gauge whether you need to upgrade.

• **Adjusting Settings:** Some games allow you to change settings for better performance. Lowering settings like texture resolution, anti-aliasing, and shadow quality can significantly boost performance if your hardware struggles with newer games.

By staying cautious and ensuring that your system can meet the demands of newer games, you can continue to enjoy a seamless gaming experience.

Maintaining and improving your gaming PC is an ongoing process that helps you get the most out of your investment. By keeping drivers updated, updating hardware as needed, and ensuring your system can handle future games, your PC will continue to provide an excellent gaming experience for years to come.

Regular updates and proper game installations also help ensure that you're always ready for the next big release, maximizing your gaming pleasure.

Chapter 9: Installing Your Preferred Game

Once your system is updated and optimized, it's time to run the games you've been eagerly waiting to play. Installing games quickly ensures that your system runs smoothly and your storage is managed properly. Here's how to install your games:

Choosing the Right Platform

The first step in installing a game is choosing the platform on which you'll buy or download it. Each platform has its own method of distribution and installation, and the most famous ones include:

- **Steam:**

The largest gaming distribution platform, offering thousands of games. Steam requires you to install its client, which then handles your game library and downloads. Once installed, you can purchase, download, and install games straight from the Steam client.

- **Epic Games Store:**

Known for giving free games and exclusive titles. Like Steam, Epic Games requires its own client, which you'll need to install before getting games.

- **GOG (Good Old Games):**

A DRM-free site that allows you to download and install games without any copy protection. GOG's Galaxy client is optional but offers an easier way to manage your game library.

- **Other Platforms:**

There are also smaller platforms such as Origin, Ubisoft Connect, and Microsoft Store that you might use based on the games you play.

Each platform requires you to make an account, and some may have extra software or services that need to be installed. After setting up the client, you're ready to start downloading your games.

Game Installation Process

Once you've chosen your platform and purchased your game, the installation process is pretty simple:

1. Launch the Platform Client: Open the client connected with the platform you're using, whether it's Steam, Epic Games Store, or another.

2. Download the Game: Navigate to your library or purchased games area. Select the game you want to install and hit the Download button. The client will immediately download the game files to your PC.

3. Choose Installation Location: Depending on how you've set up your storage, the game may load to your default drive (usually your C: drive). If you have multiple drives (for example, an SSD and an HDD), choose the drive where you want to put the game. It's a good idea to put most games on an SSD for faster load times.

The download process will vary in speed based on your internet connection, but once finished, the game will be ready to play. Some platforms also offer the option to prepare games before their official release date, so you can start playing as soon as the game goes live.

SSD Installation for Faster Performance

If you have an SSD (Solid State Drive), it's highly recommended that you put your most-played games on it. SSDs are much faster than traditional hard drives (HDDs), which means games will load faster, reducing waiting times, especially for big open-world games or graphically demanding titles.

How to Install Games on an SSD:

1. During the game installation process, when asked to choose the installation directory, select your SSD (usually labeled as "C:\" or the drive with "SSD" in the name).

2. Make sure you have enough free space on the SSD to handle the game. Most modern games can

run from 30GB to 100GB or more, so keep an eye on the available storage.

3. After installation, you'll notice significantly faster load times, texture streaming, and overall smoother gameplay compared to installing on an HDD.

If you have different storage drives, you can also set your default install location in the game client's settings to always install games on your SSD.

Managing Game Files and Storage

As you add more games, your storage space may fill up quickly, especially if you're using an SSD. It's important to manage your storage effectively to avoid running out of space:

- **Uninstall Unused Games:** Periodically check for games that you no longer play. Most platforms allow you to uninstall games with a few clicks, freeing up room for new installs.

- **Move Games Between Drives:** Some systems, like Steam, let you move games between different drives without having to redownload them. This can be useful if you're running low on SSD room but still want to keep the game on faster storage.

- **Keep Backups:** Some games can have large patches or extra content that can consume storage. Consider keeping backups of larger games or content packs on an external drive if you don't need instant access.

Now that your game is setup and optimized, you're ready to start playing. Remember that regular updates to your game platform client, as well as periodic maintenance of your storage, will keep your system working at its best.

By following these steps and best practices for installing and managing your chosen games, you ensure smooth gameplay and make the most of your gaming PC setup.

Conclusion

Congratulations! By following this guide, you've taken the first step toward building, optimizing, and maintaining your dream game PC. Whether you're a beginner or an experienced gamer, the knowledge you've learnt will help you not only enjoy the latest games with high performance but also future-proof your setup for years to come.

In this final section, we'll provide a few tips to help you get the most out of your gaming PC, as well as some final pieces of advice for optimal performance and pleasure.

The following words describe the subject:

Getting the Most Out of Your Gaming PC

To truly maximize the potential of your gaming PC, it's important to know that performance isn't just about having the most powerful hardware. The real magic happens when you've optimized both your gear and software to work together in perfect harmony. Here are some tips for making the most of your setup:

1. Regularly Update Software: Keep your OS, drivers, and game players up to date. Updates often contain important patches for speed improvements and security fixes that ensure your system runs efficiently.

2. Overclocking (When Necessary): If you're an advanced user, try overclocking your CPU or GPU to squeeze out extra performance. Just be sure to watch your system's temperature and stability during these changes to avoid overheating.

3. Maintain Your System: Keeping your PC clean and dust-free, as well as running regular diagnostics and performance tests, ensures that your gaming PC works at its peak for longer.

4. Optimize In-Game Settings: Not all games require maximum settings. For demanding games, find the balance between graphics quality and speed by adjusting in-game settings like resolution, texture quality, and anti-aliasing. This will provide a smoother game experience without overloading your system.

5. Use an SSD for Faster Load Times: Install your operating system and games on an SSD (Solid State Drive) to experience faster load times, better gameplay, and quicker file access. This will dramatically improve the general gaming experience.

6. Monitor System speed: Keep an eye on your system's speed using software like MSI Afterburner, HW Monitor, or CPU-Z. Monitoring your system will help you catch possible issues before they become bigger problems.

The following words describe the subject:

Final Tips for Optimal Performance and Enjoyment

As you get more familiar with your new gaming setup, here are some final tips to ensure your experience stays enjoyable and seamless:

1. Ergonomics Matter: Your game experience is not just about the hardware. The setup and comfort of your game area matter too. Consider an ergonomic chair, proper work height, and accessories that allow you to game for long sessions without strain.

2. Regularly Backup Your Data: Your PC's speed may be optimized, but accidents can still happen. Backup your data regularly to avoid losing your saved games, custom settings, and other important files.

3. Stay Informed: The world of gaming technology changes rapidly. Keep up with new hardware releases, software updates, and performance tweaks to ensure your PC can handle the latest and best games.

4. Enjoy the Journey: Building and maintaining a gaming PC is a constant journey. Take pride in learning, experimenting, and fine-tuning your setup to fit your personal needs. Your gaming experience will continue to grow with every tweak and upgrade.

The following words describe the subject:

Final Words

You now have the information and tools to build, optimize, and maintain your perfect gaming PC. Whether you're looking to play the latest AAA titles at high settings, modding your favorite games, or simply enjoying your go-to titles with friends, your customized gaming PC is ready to deliver. Enjoy the process, stay up to date, and most importantly, have fun with your new ultimate game setup!